By the same author:

The Sirocco Room (1991)
The Kiosk on the Brink (1993)

THE MARBLE FLY

Jamie McKendrick

Oxford   New York

OXFORD UNIVERSITY PRESS

1997

Oxford University Press, Great Clarendon Street, Oxford OX2 6DP

Oxford   New York

Athens   Auckland   Bangkok   Bogota   Bombay   Buenos Aires
Calcutta   Cape Town   Dar es Salaam   Delhi   Florence   Hong Kong
Istanbul   Karachi   Kuala Lumpur   Madras   Madrid   Melbourne
Mexico City   Nairobi   Paris   Singapore   Taipei   Tokyo   Toronto

and associated companies in
Berlin   Ibadan

Oxford is a trade mark of Oxford University Press

British Library Cataloguibg in Publication Data
Data available

Library of Congress Cataloging in Publication Data
McKendrick, Jamie, 1955–
The marble fly / Jamie McKendrick.
p.   cm.—(Oxford poets)
I. Title.   II. Series.
PR6063.C544M37   1997   821'.914—dc20   96-32271
ISBN 0-19-283256-5

1 3 5 7 9 10 8 6 4 2

Typeset by Rowland Phototypesetting Limited
Printed in Hong Kong

For Xon de Ros

ACKNOWLEDGEMENTS

I am grateful to the editors of the following newspapers and publications in which some of these poems first appeared: *Guardian*, *London Review of Books*, *New Writing 5*, *Observer*, *Oxford Poetry*, *Poetry Quarterly*, *Poetry Review*, *The Times Literary Supplement*, and in Italy *Viaggio in Italia* and *Poiesis*.

My thanks are due to the editors of two anthologies, *After Ovid: New Metamorphoses* (Michael Hofmann and James Lasdun), and *Liverpool Accents* (Peter Robinson).

With thanks also to the Cherwell County Council and Southern Arts who commissioned 'A Flight of Locks'.

CONTENTS

THE MARBLE FLY

ANCIENT HISTORY

The year began with baleful auguries:
comets, eclipses, tremors, forest fires,
the waves lethargic under a coat of pitch
the length of the coastline. And a cow spoke,
which happened last year too, although last year
no one believed cows spoke. Worse was to come.
There was a bloody rain of lumps of meat
which flocks of gulls snatched in mid-air
while what they missed fell to the ground
where it lay for days without festering.
Then a wind tore up a forest of holm-oaks
and jackdaws pecked the eyes from sheep.
Officials construing the Sibylline books
told of helmeted aliens occupying
the crossroads, and high places of the city.
Blood might be shed. Avoid, they warned,
factions and in-fights. The tribunes claimed
this was the usual con-trick
trumped up to stonewall the new law
about to be passed. Violence was only curbed
by belief in a rumour that the tribes
to the east had joined forces and forged
weapons deadlier than the world has seen
and that even then the hooves of their scouts
had been heard in the southern hills.
The year ended fraught with the fear of war.
Next year began with baleful auguries.

MATADOR

He left that bull of a man to bleed
at the dead end of the granite puzzle
and by winding spider's silk on a cotton reel
got the hell out—the first to do so, thanks
to the brute's half-sister, the mistress who'd
masterminded his escape. For reward
he took her off to Naxos, and there he dumped her.
No great shame, as anyway the wine god
had just drawn up in his leopardskin caravan
but it gives you some idea about our man.

While snapping shut the pleats of his scarlet cape
in a media veronica for the crew's applause
the last thing on his mind were those black sails.
But at landfall—the name exact—he saw
a vague figure hang in the updraft for an age
against the cliffs and waited for the noise,
dark-centred and spray-edged, to flower inside him.
Only then did the thought come home
that the death of the monster in the maze
was never the real object of his voyage.

PAESTUM

The three temples are like things with roots
that channel the weather into bedrock
and pulse with a low frequency way under earshot
earth rumours back into the stratosphere.

The uttermost limit of the Grand Tour,
its point of exhaustion and refreshment,
the travertine stonework rises like a
shimmering wall of sea although the sea

and its god have withdrawn from sight behind
the polished cubits of the perimeter wall
leaving the harbour stranded. Malaria
filled the spaces where the sea had been,

and shifting trade-routes and the tilt of power
and a black rain of lapilli
left this stone unroofed and tenantless, the haunt
by day of jackdaws and by night of owls.

Snakes that pose under the famous roses
at the edge of wedding photos last year claimed
a satin bride for Dis. The Doric columns
tower in TV adverts and tourist brochures

while the triglyphs still grip the entablature
like talons. On the diver's tomb in the museum
earth swells and might as well be water under
the silent leap of the diver

—his body finding itself in mid-flight
suddenly supple again and childlike, arched,
his weight assumed by air which any moment might
spring wide like the Sea Gate onto a burning source.

VEHICLE

I jolt awake at the wheel of this wreck
  made of resin, crystals and cracked amber,
its dashboard dial a compass pointing south.

  All the things I ever had and kept—
  old files, old coats and age-old daily papers,
smudged and piss-yellow, fly out the rear-window

    unravelling and tearing in the backdraught
    and snagging on the dark umbrella pines
that line the coast now that the rocks have turned

    to the sand we glimpse when the wood gives way
    to trees. The mozzarella buffalo are chewing
lumps of earth and barely lift their heavy heads

    to watch us. The hard shoulder's a fur-rack
    of flattened stoats and moles and the odd dog
lying among pools of oil and shattered bodywork.

  We pass the dead city with its four gates,
  three temples and twice-flowering roses;
then the one stall selling painted urns and postcards.

  A black-haired woman stands by the road
  in a tight lowcut black crape dress—
for miles the wind brings lovely skeins and pockets of

    her spikenard perfume through the former windscreen
    with flakes of darkness which we wipe away
like ash-filled cobwebs or swart veils of lace.

  And as the sun drops to the lacquered sea
  it's hard to figure out how long the car
can hold together, given the speed it's going,

or how long it's been since we set out
    trailing tiny shining cubes of glass
and scattering scraps of everything I've owned

    past so many earthworks and abandoned
    homes that now it seems I'm staring
out at the Pole Star through a window of bone.

A ROMAN RUIN

RIP Wolseley 1500, MOT
failure cum laude, rust-plaqued, cough-racked jade,
eyesore, ossiary, tin tub, dustbin
—that last oil can was your extreme unction.

What's left can be my memento mori
or a monument to Britain's now decayed
industrial base. There's a sepia postcard
bluetacked to your walnut dashboard

of the ruined palace of one Septimus
—weeds feasting off its arches much as moss
(some rolling stone) does on your window rim.

O pilgrim, you who search for Rome in Rome . . .
Forget it. Neither the Tiber nor the Thames
will be graced again by your ancient chrome.

BONESHAKER

' "Is it about a bicycle", he asked.' —Flann O'Brien

My not having read *The Third Policeman*
left the piece I'd meant to write on bicycles
seriously under-researched, to put it politely,

as you did, but even before that crucial omission
the whole idea was a non-starter given
I'd never recollect with anything like

tranquillity the strong emotion I experienced
when some sly thief under cloak of darkness
coaxed my racer from the plastic drainpipe

I'd chained it to. No matter that it cost a fiver
from a Hackney scrapyard whose curator
sat throned on an armchair which long ago

may have looked less like a padded dishrag.
Feed the cats, he growled at his thin crony
who began to saw in half an industrial can

of whalemeat while their nine cats, nine lives apiece,
that's as many as eighty-one lives, converged on him
like a raddled orchestra of shofars.

I saw the bike at once and lifted it sky-high
with the distal phalanx of my little finger.
It was as light as a bird not as a feather

like Valéry suggested the true poem should be.
Its lightness was such that it must have been stolen
even then, or especially then, but I eyed it

as Phaeton must have eyed his father's chariot.
I can see you're straight up, the man told my friend
and then (as if aware he'd left me out)

I'm not saying that you're a villain.
But wheels don't come as narrow as those wheels are.
You could pawn that pushbike in a piss-hole.

Eh? Without more words I paid hard cash
but the next day going down the Ball's Pond Road
on that brace of shakes with its shaky brakes

I achieved an unrehearsed forwards roll
across a windscreen the way those Cretan girls
would flip over the horns of a bull, which as

Picasso noticed were the shape of handlebars
but that story's been told. One life later,
the man who'd scythed me down was whistling:

The speed you were going was more like the wind
than the wind itself, an image
he must have known would more than make amends

for the fact that the bike was never quite the same
with a crotchety click at its cotter-pin
and a kerbward-biased front wheel which wore down

one breakblock like a shauchled heel though still
it was fleet as Achilles and a sight less warlike,
being one of mankind's few benign inventions

though the truth is I can't help but hope
it's been far from benign to the one who stole it.
May he bruise his shins—ouch—on those pedals.

for Bernard O'Donoghue

THE SPLEEN FACTORY

(after Carlos Drummond de Andrade)

I want to make a sonnet that's not a sonnet
according to any civilized notion of what
that is. I want it ugly as concrete,
and just about impossible to read.

And I'd like my sonnet in the future
to give no living soul an ounce of pleasure,
not by being merely foulmouthed and perverse
but also (why not?) by being both and worse

if it feels the urge. Plus I want the whole thing caustic
and obtrusive—with intent to pierce and hurt
like stitches done without anaesthetic

somewhere tender. So it won't be learnt by heart.
So it's a wall with a hole pissed through—in the hole a star
transmitting incomprehensible clarity.

THE ONE-STAR

Moving away in the taxi, I could just see myself
   climbing the marble steps and stepping through
   the plate-glass into a lounge-cum-vestibule,

its floor inlaid with a pink star of mineral grains
   and roughage—a breakfast for the after-life.
   Beaded oak cladding, electrified oil-lamps.

a pharaonic desk-clerk. The air was cut and dried
   as though reconstituted in the basement's lungs
   and laid out, and folded, in cool dry reams.

The Shining was obtainable on the video service
   but would be scrambled after several minutes
   if you failed to press the 'Confirm' button

—otherwise it was a sex film I was embarrassed
   for the glamorous Thai receptionist
   to know I was watching. So I tried to read

The Temptation to Exist feeling conspicuously
   absent and uneasily aware
   of being ironed flat, flatter, by the clean sheets

and of the bedside table's inbuilt clock
   with its defective digits: every minute
   was a minus sign or a gnomon, every hour

was missing a slant side to its parallelogram.
   I closed the eyelids of the two nightlights;
   then mine . . . until I woke as though I'd feasted

on finely-ground enamel. There was nothing for it
   but to go home—some home!—but first why not
   spirit away the bar of opalescent soap, the small

urn of bath-foam and the shroud-sewing kit
    the size of a matchbook, with loops of thread
    five different shades of grey

or maybe it was the light? I had a good mind
    to mend the inside lining of my coat
    but instead went down in the shiny lift

and sank in an armchair by the crystal ashtray.
    Was I a Mr John Ashbery, someone asked me.
    No, I replied, not Mr Ashbery

—but pausing mysteriously mid-sentence as I felt
    he deserved a couple more guesses for being
    somehow on the right track, if not exactly warm.

The pause obviously disturbed him. He didn't
    like that pause. Well tell him
    if you'd be so kind that his taxi's waiting.

Oh yes I could just see myself doing that.

for Michael Hofmann

THE MARBLE FLY

The guide crinkled his nose
like a squirrel with a nut
as he pointed out to us
the baked-clay phallus
on the oven door, no doubt
symbolic of the risen loaf.

Red dust and stone thresholds
to an unrecovered world,
stone fruit that Felix
the fruitseller sold, stone-cold
drinks from the hot drinks stall,
wheel ruts cut in the stone road.

Murals, mosaics, mysteries:
the pierced stag, the girl's back
exposed to the beaded whip,
a lion mauling the shift of Thisbe
whilst a wall-eyed Pyramus
has severed an artery.

A wall relief in the Wool Market
shows the animal world in marble
—a lizard canopening a cricket,
a mouse airlifted by an owl
and a fly (watch out, fly!)
on its own among the bulrushes—

all perfectly preserved and just
a shade larger than lifesize
and much stiller than life and harder.
It can't have been long after
that much the same idea
occurred to Vesuvius.

SPAN

Eye-level with the alps of ash and slag
I trawl my floor for a BT counterfoil
deep into its scarlet monitory phase
through shards and rags and scraps
and rivelled gold tobacco threads and these
long white hairs which must be mine
alas as no one else
would venture into this rented room
except one short-haired black-haired cat.
And here's a flea he carried on his back,
a tiny emissary from the caliphat
of bad dreams, doing vaults and back-flips
onto three golden dusters, bought last year
and still sealed in polythene,
their hems blanket-stitched with crimson thread
in a series of small 'v's overlapping
the dictionary. Crimson: it burns a fuse
the length of a dusty trail of roots
back to Arabic: qirmizi:
meaning the Scarlet Grain insect which breeds
on the kermes oak—stuff Solomon hung
beneath the wrought-gold
five-cubit wingspan of the cherubim . . .
crimson lights up back along the line of
the trade-routes west, at each camel-stop
or port—a vowel-shift, a letter
dislodged from the throat to the palate
colouring the sound. My eyes lift
to the level of the window, facing east
onto brickwork, tarmac and slate tiles.
Upon the window-sill—a fly's black torso,
deep in the mire of last year's dust,
with its seraph wings still poised for flight
but cumbersome like panes
of leaded glass or paddles of cracked quartz,
tired for a while of beating at the air.

THE DUET

From the eaves of the room I live in
comes a din as parliamentary and relentless
as windscreen wipers on a dry windscreen
—tremulous ballads to domestic bliss
which rarely get beyond the first failed line.
But then the clatter of my electric Canon,
its pinhead headbutting the daisywheel,
will stop them gargling gravel for a while.

It's at it again, their silence might be saying,
it's nature's joke the way those creatures sing.
And, as hardly ever, if it should go on
over the page an indignant pigeon,
that's my excuse, rakes the gutter with its claws
and creaks into flight like a rusty hinge.

FLIGHT

spruce hickory bamboo
(though only for a few seconds)
the first aircraft flew

as if the wind had a mind
to clear the air of any weather
that might tilt the scales
one way or the other

as the tenons quaked
and the dowelling screaked
and the single rear rudder

came to grief
like the tail
or tailfeather
of an unfledged hippogriff.

for Valerie Lipman

17

FLYING COLOURS

In a terracotta field in Catalonia
I help a small boy set his kite aloft
though neither of us has a notion how
it's meant to work, the wind—the tramontana that lifts

the white dust from the hoofmarks on the dirt-track
and crinkles an earthbound beetle's wingcase
after vaulting the peaks of the Pyrenees—
knows enough for both of us and hoiks

the heraldic disc with its long tail of cellophane
out and up, taut then slack then taut once more,
unlooping the nylon cord which at a certain
height vanishes into thin air like gossamer

and the boy calls out ¡mira la cometa como va!
though it looks to me like it needs
a new name—not kite, not comet . . . some odd idea
happily going nowhere in a series of nods

swerves, shrugs, juts, rips, spins and figures-of-eight
so, unsure which is near or far, or up or down,
he and I are nothing but the place the kite
has chosen us to anchor on

as gusts riffle the sweetcorn's papery sheaves
and pluck at the kermes oaks and pylon wires
and we marvel at the tiny planet attached to us
—its jagged flight,

                    its deep unearthly colours.

A FLIGHT OF LOCKS

i *Flow*

The Greek who said you can never
step into the same river
twice hadn't dreamt of

the slow seepage of canals
with their oil and graphite sheen,
liquid packed solid as a pencil lead

where time is cased in a long cabinet
stowed with the ownerless archives
of two centuries of weather,

the lump of coal from Warwickshire,
the tipcat, the fender, the bleached horse's tail
once tied to a painted tiller.

ii *Canal*

The wheels of perpetual motion
have ground to a halt
or almost a halt

while underwater on the bed
of puddled clay
packhorses trod down watertight

in that sedgy trench of slime
lies the frayed peak of a navvy's cap
beside a copper

cartwheel twopenny-bit, its rim
incised with 1 7 9 7
around the frogspawn jowls of George the Third.

iii *Canalside*

The fishers sit beside
the giant on its back
with their chests-of-drawers

packed with quills of peacock, crow
and porcupine for floats and bait
of maggots, casters, hempseed, wheat

hearing the water's sluggish flow
like a flywheel ticking, a lunar tug
from the summit down the flight of locks

to the headwaters of the tidal river
—quiet as the perch's crimson fin
that surfaces and disappears.

iv *Lock*

At the crank of the windlass in the racks
the paddle boards' square blocks of elm
are lifted in the lock head like two eyelids

so water sluices through the culverts
on either side of the lock's brick chamber
in swags and scallops and volutes

burled and blurred and bossed and scooped
like a crystal maelstrom in a bottleneck
crizzling its uprush in a double ridge

till risen it overrides itself
and the sky resembles its reflection
on the stilled upheaval of one level.

v *Heron*

Dead-centre down the still canal
a blue ghost flies with a mussel shell
clamped lightly in its bill

folding the daybreak's river mist
with the creaking steps of its flight
past the diamonds and daisies on the cratch

of the narrowboat
clove-hitched to a cast-iron bollard,
past the dredger's hopper, the humpbacked bridge

then drops the empty shell
still hinged by a thread
among flints and ashkeys on the tow-path.

vi *Bridge*

The humpbacked bridge
is taking umbrage
and making a bright hoop

of its bricklined arch
like a dancer's sturdy instep
on the unbroken surface

where the quilled stumps
of pollard willows
shiver like the steel bristles

on a flea's armour
or rest, head-down, like sable
brushes in a jar of turps.

IN THE HOLD

Route-marching, field-postcards, tents hung with scrim
—we waited in those Domesday parishes
for D-Day to begin.

Beyond the wood there was a flint-harled church
and a watertower like a missile in plainclothes
— a tall tube with a concrete hat on top.

I can still feel the pink rim the beret left
embossed on my receded hairline
and the veins in my forehead swelling

with the notes of the bird I couldn't see
bubbling like water through a sea-vent
while darkness linked the leaves and thickened.

From Suffolk they drove us down by night
to the New Forest where we were nearer still
the zero-hour

that months of training had prepared us for
not thinking too far ahead of or about
by filling the days with strict inspections.

And then the lorry drive in convoy
to the blunt-hulled landing ships,
the gangplank a small step from the footboard.

Once in the hold I heard the air compress
as the round steel hatch was clamped down shut
and tightened by a half-turn on the hand-grips

and there we all were in the dim light that came on
stowed in the hollow belly of the war
—a box that clanged and stank of diesel—

till daylight heaped us on the other shore.

ULTIMA THULE

On a family outing to the final island,
wobblingly tall, the fools of ocean, together
we rode the rubber dinghy. Our father manned

the stunted paddles, blade on the feather,
regardless of the waves chilled from world's end.
The black octagonal basalt columns reared

like a row of crayons worn down at different
rates from scribbling on the ether,
the nearest—pedestals for cormorants.

Like weathervanes, the rowlocks slithered round.
The boat floor pumped and tussled like a heart
sculpting our insteps with its upthrust as

the island rowed itself away from us
towering at the edge of time forever.

BANANA BOAT

'I wasn't born on a banana boat yesterday'
the porter told us (not that we'd asked)
when we tried to bluff our way without a pass
into the Liverpool University Pool.
He growled then waved us through the turnstyle
with a wink as good as a season ticket.
Did he know me from somewhere, or just think he did?

As for me, I wasn't born in a bungalow.
I was, come to think of it—not so much born
as put together, the main piece fitting into place
when we moved to a house above the Mersey
and the concrete rampart of Garston Docks,
the barbed-wire and the pill-box from the war
—the main piece, or so I'd like to think.

But if Pat Cassidy wasn't born, as he said
he wasn't, on one of Fyffe's banana boats
which from the Albert Dock used to supply
the whole country with bananas (except during the war)
that didn't rule out he might have been born
on some other boat like a vessel stacked
with iron-bound trunks of Swedish pine

on their way to be axed into matchsticks
at Bryant & May's factory down the road,
or in the hold of a ship from Trinidad
full of sugar cane for Tate & Lyle's.
Certainly there was something
scouse-maritime about him—an old hulk
moored to a sandbank on the river.

He made me think of the one heirloom I had
(from my mother's father I'd never met)—
a Bermuda-rig model yacht plank-built
by Mr Rawlinson, his friend, the docker,
and of the foghorns' shindy on New Year's Eve
when the boat-lights blazed at the stroke of twelve
where Sassoon had dumped his Military Cross.

Still, whether on one or another sort of boat,
at sea or in dry dock, no one would dispute
that Corporal Cassidy, who had (I found out)
served beside my father in the Second,
admittedly, and not the First World War
—no one would dispute he wasn't born yesterday
though his cheeks were as pink as if he was.

SURVIVAL

as the crew sang
a capstan shanty
adapted by
Barbadians
from an Irish tune

the ten-gun brig
hove to
beside a cherty rock
in mid-Atlantic
only occupied

by crabs and lichen
and nesting colonies
of the booby
and the noddy
—*of such a tame*

and stupid disposition
the naturalist recalled
I could have killed
any number of them
with my geological hammer

—there in a nutshell
he'd hit on
the origin
of the Origin
and the twilight of Species

TAKEN AWARES

I fall into every trap
they set for me—
mantrap, mousetrap, birdlime.

Every time
I take the bait—
the worm, the cheese, whatever.

I pluck the wire
that shifts the lever
that springs the teeth.

Then, in the calm before death,
I flatter myself
I'd seen it all a mile off.

I even manage a small laugh.

SIX CHARACTERS IN SEARCH
OF SOMETHING

A friend of mine met the son of a man
who it seems was eaten by a polar bear
in Iceland where the bear had stepped ashore
rafted from Greenland on an ice-floe.

The father of the man who met my friend
saw the bear who'd eat him loitering near
the shore and hurried on and met another man
who was walking the other way towards the bear.

He gave that other man his walking stick
but the bear meanwhile had doubled back
and reappeared on the path ahead
of the man who now was unprotected.

There may be a moral in this story
for the man, his son, the man he met,
for my friend, for me, or even for the bear,
but if there is it's better left unsaid.

THE BEST OF THINGS

The lawn wears
a peaked hat
—that'll be

the velvet fellow
brisking with his claws
through the dark shaft

one worm dipped
in strychnine
the farmer said

would do for him
and his whole tribe:
he eats the worm

drops dead
underground then
his brother eats him

dies and so on
till the last one chews
through the last but one

maybe out of respect
like those people
in New Guinea

dying from kuru
after eating
other people

(nature knows best)
or maybe it's just
waste not want not

that'll be it
—digging away there—
have a nice day

BRAIN MUSIC

The Beware sign pops up in the frontal cortex
like a piece of toast to the sound-effect
of a plucked gutstring and a plastic kazoo.

Don't try eating that piece of toast,
it's ghostly food, webbed with horsehair and pale
as plaster which the fingernail of dread

is writing on. What's happened, brain?
It's just a postcard. The quick flippery noise
of it catching in the slot then coming free

to rustle on the floor and, yes, the cold waft
of air could take you by surprise
I suppose but it's not like

Mephistopheles has dropped in
his gilt-edged visiting-card, it's not
quite the occasion to go sending off

frantic missives down the wires
to the body's outposts. Oh so you've read it
too, you've been putting eyes to work?

Seems a nice enough sort of message to me.
An imminent visit of a close old friend?
And there's a picture of a pretty foreign town.

You didn't even look at that. Anyone would think
you'd just spotted a centipede heading straight
for your deep equator, its little legs

a shade redder than the rest of it but moving
quite balletically without the help
of anything remotely like you.

That's better now, stop blowing on that absurd
kazoo, think of something slow and rustic,
a ceramic ocarina, or upbeat if you must

like cajun zydeko, leave heart alone
—she's got work enough to do without
your network of electrical tantrums

to cope with. She's on her last legs as it is.
Now why are you making arms stuff things
into that case? Arms have got their own things

to do like making cigarettes to keep you happy
even though heart doesn't like them in the least,
in fact apart from you no one does though they're all

prepared to put up with them just for a little calm
—at considerable risk to their own safety—
and this horrid music's all they get from you.

NAME-TAG

Every sock and collar has a name-tag.
I have a name, a surname, and a tartan rug
with tassels. What else? A zip-up
pigskin letterwriting-case that's pitted
where the bristles have been scorched away.
Once a week we write neat letters home with
our marks and team scores which the master reads.
Mornings, we get a tick for shitting
after the prefect has inspected it.
Through the keyhole old MacMillan
is sitting on his single bed
and talking to the service revolver
he uses with blanks to start the races.
Our toes are fat red bulbs from chilblains.
Already one skin has rubbed away, another grown
harder than the first, a kind of pigskin.
We must never sneak or blub or suck up.
We wear steel studs that spark. Scoured lugs
stick out from crew cuts as we learn by heart
the Latin for pitching camp and waging war
and the psalm where I am made
to lie down in green pastures and a table
is prepared for me and my enemies.
The tables are mopped with swab rags,
the dustbins tipped among the ferns
and bamboo of the watergarden
for this was once a Country House
and we are lucky to enjoy the fine grounds
which we see through the barred windows
or on Sunday walks trying to keep up
with the master who ran the marathon.
In the wooden locker by the metal bed
I have a chipped enamel mug,
a toothbrush, a comb, a nailbrush and two shoebrushes
with which, with time, I could scrub away
my shoes, my nails, my hair, my teeth—

given time enough, the buildings, the pitches,
the gate's ironwork with its clawing lion
and all we've learnt till nothing's left
but the Blasted Oak I carved my name on
and perhaps the derelict pavilion.

PERSON UNKNOWN

It remembers me still the time I left
with a kilim bag sewn to a hessian strip

which held the fresh pad and the pen-knife to cut
a reed pen from a bed of bulrushes

and for the time being the one pyramid
bottle of waterproof Chinese Stick ink

inside. Since then has anything occurred
to change the shapes I meant to make?

I passed an unknown person on the road
wearing red shoes with coiled rope soles.

The ink dried mauve in tiny alps of grit.
The knife broke. The book yellowed. The bag frayed

holding on by a few plumed threads
then snapped and left my shoulders set

and warped against the phantom weight
of thin air that hasn't forgotten me yet.

SOMEWHERE PLEASE

Nowadays not so much I don't know why
maybe we don't care for company or dread
the beggar with the dagger at our throat

but then it was done with a thumb or a sign
ideally where they could or had to slow
a sliproad a roundabout or layby

you'd follow the heft of your sack up
into the cabin and watch the asphalt splay below
or the wipers try to clean it clean it

at your right would sit the shaved ex-wrestler
the HGVman done for GBH
who mentions the three youths in the nightclub

who made a big mistake
and fell through an upstairs window backwards
for their pains—it seems he'd still

like to get his hands on the magistrate
that sent him down—the very hands
which tighten round the tiny steering wheel

as though to plunge it through the chassis
or pluck it like a daisy . . . but he knows
you're on his side and he's regretful

that now he has to turn off so he drops you
beside a field which grows an endless crop
of nothing the look of liver pâté combed

and in no time a Latvian reins his van into the layby
and tells you of the beings from a star
beyond our telescopes who minister

to his petrol supply—they are stern but kindly
and have our interests at heart or at
the jewelled pump which serves them for a heart

his abstruser claims are authorised
by longish Latin quotes and there's a prayer
he knows can change meat into vegetable

since Abel died for eating flesh . . .
now it's dark and you're standing somewhere like
Scotch Corner—let's call it double-dark—midway

along the journey of our life you feel
you've not advanced an inch or else
some smiling Zeno's engineered your route

the headlights lighthouse past you without time
or thought to read never mind admire
your cross-hatched serifs in black biro

and that strip of cardboard what does it smell of?
bananas so your guess is that
it's used to travelling—if the next car stops

if not the next the next one after that
you'll leave it there to ornament the kerb

GAINFUL EMPLOYMENT

As if I had nothing better to do,
and who says I have, than putting the house
I haven't got in order, I sit at the oak desk
I have got, though really a table not a desk
but it's mine and I sanded it down myself
and beeswaxed it with iron wire-wool

—that was how important it was for me:
this surface on which so much was to be
accomplished. Best of all, I can take
its legs off, and replace them by way of
four angelic wing-nuts to the corner brackets
so it's both a steadfast and a movable beast.

But I wonder why I kept this biro spring
I'm exercising now between my finger
and thumb—not to sew my eyelids up with
like the envious spirits in purgatory.
Just too exquisite to throw away,
an image of infinity or information . . .

I'm still here, where there's an unconsolable
joy to be had, sitting ready at my station
and waiting for the bugle or the slughorn.
No one can say it's wasting time, my time, the time I've got
to enter the very thread of the helix,
to live always expecting the unheard of.

ILLUMINATED MANUSCRIPT

The Master of the Entangled Figures
has penned me in the curl of a worm's tail,
a weirdly ribbed and beaded spiral
inside the U of the word VIR
at the head of The Book of Job's first verse.
Soon as I'd set foot in the Land of Uz
I watched him bite his tongue to stop it
rushing ahead of the script, a laborious
thicket of Latin in which each capital
is pressed out like blue from a stone. No doubt
I'll come to accept my entanglement
like a mute owl on an ivy tod
though now I can hardly tell
where my limbs begin and his letters end.

POSSESSION

This patch of green attached to the rented house
belongs to the clutches of the ivy
I've begun (what's got into me?)
to rip from the sycamore trunk it's clamped on
and from the lawn where its cables,
like supply-lines, are dug in
through bronchial roots, and bear an iron code:
extend, secure. It tears the skin from my fingers,
expressing a thin milk, probably poison.
In one afternoon, I've undone seasons
of reinforcement, of slow dominion
as though I had a new law to dispense.

As though I had some hanging-gardens in mind.
But the verminous life-forms it's helped
advance: spiders, woodlice and snails that creep,
at their respective paces, back and away
in search of cover. The earth itself
seems dank and affronted, and a death's-head moth
foxes my eyelids like a page of Euclid
—all painted dust, bristling and admonitory.
Soon enough I'll be tangled up like Laocoön
on the compost heap, my wrists and ankles bound,
and the small creatures will be at home in me
and my mouth will sprout a glossy angular leaf.

A SHORTENED HISTORY IN PICTURES

The Child Maximilian in a White Frock.
The Imperial Family with their Chairs and Pet Cat.
Maximilian, a Thoughtful Young Man in Black.
Maximilian, Emperor of Mexico, at Court.
The Empress of Mexico, his Wife Charlotte.
The Emperor Maximilian on Horseback.
Maximilian and his Court Playing Cricket
(with the English Ambassador, Sir Charles Wyke).

The Broken Cacti and the Convent's Outer Wall.
The Execution Squad Standing to Attention.
A Mestizo Leading a Llama under Popocatépetl.
The Execution of Miramón, Mejía and Maximilian.
The Gold-Green Tail-Feathers of the Quetzal.
The Emperor's Shirt after his Execution.

THE CENTURY PLANT

A century after its introduction
to Oxford's Botanical Gardens greenhouse,
on the site of the medieval Jewish cemetery,
the agave has taken a leap of faith
it won't survive, and begun to blaze
with sulphurous buds. It's not clear whether
global or more local warming lit the fuse
in the patient rootstock and sent one limb
rocketing upward so its top
can look down even on the banana tree
besides the other transplants. The palm-line
is said to move a metre north each year
—these days more like a kilometre—
but either way the agave's too far ahead
to be caught up with, despite the hundred years
of waiting—now two, at the most three weeks
of prodigal flowering and the whole thing ends.

In 1850 in Seville,
while his contemporaries photographed
rotting barges on the Guadalquivir
or farm labourers in sheepskin waistcoats
or Gypsy women in the tobacco factory,
Vicomte J. de Vigier,
turned his back on the folkloric and his lens
on the common-or-garden naturalized exotics
like palm trees and bamboo. His masterpiece,
Etude d'aloès, shows this tumid
dusty plant on a nondescript roadside.
It holds grimly on to its patch of nowhere
and drinks and drinks the silver nitrate light
as though there were no belonging anywhere
but there and then, and nothing sublime
except that stretch of dirt, that broken wall
and the rays of a faded nineteenth-century sun.

GARDENER'S WORLD

Yes, we're in the potting-shed again this week
with Mr Jones among the seedlings . . .
his wrinkles have dug in, his intellectual fingers
are a dark pollen-coated mothy umber.
He's in, he's always in, his overcoat
which when he moves gives off a sweetened cloud
of twine and potash like a hardware store.

The owners of the garden where he works
have kept a special mug for his own use
called Jonesies Mug, though no one else
would dream of using it. He sips the tea,
the florid healthy colour of flowerpots,
while muttering to the calyx of a small tomato:
Well, the Missis is a bit under the weather today.

—A figure of speech that falls a fraction short.
Right now she's barricading their front door
with thousands of cans of catfood
she'd stockpiled in the cellar against
the years of famine. He shrugs and walks away
like a dazed tortoise in the stiff panels
of his coat then stoops into the boiler-house

which stores his various implements besides
an unexplained medicine-ball like a prize pumpkin.
His cup of tea has turned as cold as stone.
And now he's ambled way beyond the rockery.
And now he's gone—the cracked furry boots
and the creases of his pass-the-parcel face
are lost forever out among the lupins.

SEISMOGRAPH COMPANY

You wouldn't survive a week with another crew
—Arthur had just broken the silence

he'd built between us since I'd first arrived.
Then the boss hauled me in for breaking

one of their precious brass-tipped poles
And no, I couldn't work with someone else.

Though slowly Arthur did relent, his grey beard
grew less hackled and his rage gave way

to an extraordinary bounty, gifts
each day: a teazle, a horseshoe, a rabbit's tail,

some foul home-brewed chocolate cinzano in a Tizer bottle,
a Cornish pasty roasted on a bonfire

stoked with a stick of dynamite,
instructions in body-building and the names of trees

and daily instalments of his life history
from steeplejack to crofter to jack-of-all-trades

—a fall from high estate to these hard times
toting a sack of fuses round the fields.

It was like he'd found in me a kind of disciple
(who'd never know the meaning of work)

or even a scribe who might yet learn to write
and in himself the gift of speech.

THE EMBRACE

(after Valerio Magrelli)

As you lie beside me I edge closer
taking sleep from your lips
as one wick draws flame from another.
And two night-lights are lit
as the flame takes and sleep passes
between us. But as it passes
the boiler in the basement shudders:
down there a fossil nature burns,
down in the depths prehistory's
sunken fermented peats blaze up
and slither through my radiator.
Wreathed in a dark halo of oil,
the bedroom is a close nest
heated by organic deposits,
by log pyres, leafmash, seething resins . . .
And we are the wicks, the two tongues
flickering on that single Palaeozoic torch.

ON/OFF

The switch stuck through the lampstand's neck
like an arrow shaft of walrus ivory
in a Welsh epic
has lost its feathers and its head.
Peacock feathers and a gold head.
Its Fiat Lux
with a length of flex,
its shift, its crick has made me
blink like a lemur at the lack
of the moon or a star
or a thing between. But it's good
how someone takes off their earrings
with the motion of shelling a pea.
A tiny snap. Like the hasp-click
of a calyx
at the press of a picker's thumb.
A sound like lifting an airtight lid
or a pin dropping in a pyramid.
Then the lobe's set free
and breathes with delight
to shed the slight weight
of the earrings.
Earrings that might be
twin filaments, a pair of ball-bearings
or a hammock-faced moon and a tarnished star.

APHRODISIACS

The lengths I'd have gone to to lead you down
the Donegal cliffs to that grass-covered ledge
—the width of us—above the Atlantic.
No one would have seen us but apparently
that wasn't the point—the point was
it was over between us and you couldn't
pretend. That night, though, in the rented bed,
for peace of mind or for old times' sake,
you must have thought, Why not. Why not indeed.
For a start because it seems you'd catch
something I caught from someone by mistake
—suddenly at sea on her wine-coloured carpet
after eating several Chinese sweets
made from fine-textured black bean-paste.

GULF

Two funerals in the one day were too much
to meet with without feeling life had some such
designs on us—both proceeding at the same pace
to within a stone's throw of the same place.
The women they passed all crossed their hearts
with a sign to divide them into quarters
while the men touched their crotches to avert
whatever it was made the dead inert.

A priest who flicked a palm frond led the first
up through the village to the place of rest:
Dives, the caterer, in a black, gilded hearse
drawn by a dazzling scarab of a horse
horned with black-azure plumes. Then came Lazarus
carried past on the fishermen's shoulders
down to the shore where his weight was lowered
for the sea to lay its cold hand on the wood.

LEGACIES

It was in the cellar of the Edinburgh house
owned by my great great grandfather

that the bodysnatchers, Burke & Hare,
unknown to him, kept their cache of corpses

in cold storage before delivering them
to the School of Human Anatomy.

There was always a skeleton in the closet,
or a skull at least, perched among the army berets,

the Luger, the greatcoat, the Zeiss binoculars
and the fox stole with its red glass eyes

and blackened lips which fastened with a snap.
There was always the skull in the clothes cupboard

with a fidgety script on its fontanel,
saying nothing, its eyes reduced to zeroes.

*

In today's newspaper I read of a Xhosa chief
who believed his great great uncle's skull was kept

somewhere in Scotland. After leaving several
military museums empty-handed,

he had a dream of a field and a white horse
grazing. In the field a barn, in the barn

that skull. And there it seems he found it
—on a shelf among some tarnished bridles—

identified by a bullet hole in the temple
from a British rifle. So some day soon

may we now expect a visit from a man
with or without a leopardskin and flywhisk

who has travelled across two continents to ask
what we've kept all this time in our closet?

ZEROES

As cunning as the steel-shod flea from Tula,
my wristwatch has a web drawn on its dial
—each hour is equal to one radial
while a black spider with a juddery pulse patrols
the web's circumference, always too late
to meet the shadow it hovers over
but consuming each second with a sated quiver.

Out beyond Earth's atmosphere, on Skylab,
for weeks they observed how several orb-web
spiders would cope with zero gravity.
Not well at first: their webs sheer gobbledygook.
They had to learn their weight meant nothing
by Bruce-like trial and error until
at last their webs were perfectly symmetrical

unlike on Earth where perfect webs would crash
without extra buttressing below.
But there, in the absence of flies, they fashioned
their nets into a heaven of pure ornament
and waited patiently for their reward.
—A flaw in the design lets the spirit escape,
as Spider woman taught the Navajo.

I never find that small trapdoor in time.
Here on my wrist the spider time draws in
the toughest substance of the natural world
and morning noon and night till zero hour
keeps casting her silk out over nothingness.
She quivers on a canny perspex disc
and flies without wings into inner space.

GALATEA AND POLYPHEMUS

(after Ovid)

I think of the sheer foulness of Polyphemus
and then of the face of Acis which seems
unfair, it's so flawless. I lay all day
in his arms on a high green sheltered ledge
hidden from the Cyclops, that one horrid eye
molten with inflammation and fixated
on my image. I hate to think of my image
pinned down in each of his pitifully few
brain cells like a doll madonna stuck
in some wall shrine lit by a grey-pink bulb
on an alley of rats and gore and filth.
His outside's bad enough—hard ulcerated
slime a loathsome cindery mauve, his one eye
like an anus, a blob, a fronded jellyfish.
Then we heard him coming and watched him squat
on a jagged promontory, the waves matting
the pelt on his calves. He sets down that stick
tall as a ship's mast and starts puffing
at a pipe of giant reeds like a church organ.
I remember his song which went like this:

O Galatea tiny-featured as a chaffinch,
supple and slender as a rowan sapling,
smooth as Greek yogurt, as jasper beads,
silkier than the inside of an oyster
—like a secret tree in the middle of the wood
casting a violet shadow. Your breasts are
like new-made planets in the night sky
which make the stars drop from the firmament
to cluster round your feet like leaves on fire
—you fit so exactly into your skin
your small chiselled joints must be transparent . . .

I'll spare you some salacious details
of how he spied me bathing naked
—my breasts like bells of flesh, my nipples
parting the water . . . his voice all thick and hectic
though bits of his song weren't actually so bad.
That's why I remember it. I wouldn't mind
Acis pirating a few of those lines
but he more than makes up for that lack
with the lines of his profile—even his wrists,
even his callussed heels are aphrodisiac
though his phrasing leaves something to be desired.
Cyclops then roughened his song with a lot of reproaches:

But, O Galatea, you're harder-hearted than gnarled oak,
falser than water, more slippery than ice,
vainer than peacocks and colder than the winter sea.
Worst of all and what I hate the most are
your sudden turns of speed in spurning me.
I'd bask in your other faults if I could just
once grab hold of you. Then see if you'd escape.
And think of all the things you're missing by not
being mine: all this mountainside, that plain
as far as those squalid dinky coast resorts
that spoil the view—I'll paste them with a layer
of mud and ash as soon as I feel myself again.
Think of the orchards bowed down with pears,
pale grapes and also black ones; my caves
uncannily tuned to body heat no matter
what season's abroad, dog days or Arctic blasts;
woodland fruits beside freshwater streams,
clumps of white-domed mushrooms, tall forests
of chestnuts, flocks of goats whose udders drip
with finest milk from which I make
clean curds by adding rennet. Are you mad?
Can't you see what I'm offering? I won't dull
your eyes with presents from the cornershop,

chocolates and daffodils—no diamanté jewels
like that cheapskate Acis gets to pin on you.
I'd dig rare gems out of the mountainside
with strange faults of fire like constellations
and fashion a necklace of dragonflies
and teach two tame owls to sing for you;
I'd twist curious lamps out of raw iron
to light you down the corridors of cave
to a bed of hoopoe crests where you would wait
for me to appear, my face dark with desire . . .
but you hate my face—it makes you cringe away.
So who says I'm that gruesome? I saw myself
in a blue pool today and thought—just look
at the size of him will you? Even Jove
who doesn't exist could never be bigger.
Does being hairy have to mean I'm vile?
Would you want a bald hound or horse, or a bird
without feathers? And if it's my one eye,
my uncompanioned eye, that bugs you what about
the sun? Two of them up there and we'd be flayed.
My eye grows on a single stem and follows
only you with its one shaft of devotion.
As for the muck on me, the stink, I'll scrub
myself with pumice every night before
we touch. Every night to touch you! O
Galatea, drop that skinny runt of an Acis
or let me at him and I'll tear his limbs
off his hairless trunk and fry them in Etna
whose channels of sulphur and blue fire
are coursing through my veins for love of you.
A love that scalds me and stops me working.
Take a look at my neglected flock. Entire fleets
pass by unscathed as if I were a lighthouse.
I just forget to wreck them. My whole life
is in arrears, in ruins like a great city
turned to burnt earth and swamps and column stumps

while all you do is quiver with disgust
at my offers and take to your exquisite heels
before I can quieten down my heartbeat
enough to speak let alone find the right words,
soft words, to let me creep closer . . .

                                        raucous
and needled by his own song, he stood up
and happened to spy us—the tongue of Acis
making waves through me without the use of words
when the rocks trembled with the Cyclops's cry
'That's the last you'll ever taste of love'.
I dived in the bay but my poor Acis
still crouched in a daze, he couldn't move as
Cyclops hefted up a rock and hurled it
crushing him, its edge alone sufficient
to flatten him. Blood trickled out from under
like autumn streams dyed coppery with leaf-juice
and the dense mass of rock, as though through guilt,
cracked open and a tall green reed sprang up
and waters gushed through the hollow rock
and a new youth waded out mid-stream,
his temples crowned in a wreath of rushes,
the waters round him whispering his name.

OXFORD POETS

Fleur Adcock
Moniza Alvi
Joseph Brodsky
Basil Bunting
Tessa Rose Chester
Daniela Crăsnaru
Michael Donaghy
Keith Douglas
D. J. Enright
Roy Fisher
Ida Affleck Graves
Ivor Gurney
David Harsent
Gwen Harwood
Anthony Hecht
Zbigniew Herbert
Tobias Hill
Thomas Kinsella
Brad Leithauser
Derek Mahon
Jamie McKendrick

Sean O'Brien
Alice Oswald
Peter Porter
Craig Raine
Zsuzsa Rakovszky
Christopher Reid
Stephen Romer
Eva Salzman
Carole Satyamurti
Peter Scupham
Jo Shapcott
Penelope Shuttle
Goran Simić
Anne Stevenson
George Szirtes
Grete Tartler
Edward Thomas
Charles Tomlinson
Marina Tsvetaeva
Chris Wallace-Crabbe
Hugo Williams